THE QUESTING SELF

The Questing Self

BY RUTH RUSSELL DAVIS

Alved of Detroit, Incorporated

1948

Published by

ALVED OF DETROIT, INCORPORATED

500 Buhl Building, Detroit 26

Manufactured in the United States of America

To

J. R. D.

For all your
patience and understanding.

THE CONTENTS

THE QUESTING SELF

Rabboni, Why?

"Lazarus, come forth!"
The cry resounded sharp, imperative,
One that could not be denied,
And it to which the call was made
Stirred, and shook with grievous pain.
There was no light, no sound,
No change in gloom nor silence of the tomb,
And yet the cry was light and blinding light,
And awesome noise; a something felt
That lit the darkness of that quarried vault
To radiance intangible, undeniable, unseen;
A thunder loud as breakers of all earthly seas
Which bade the spirit fled to quicken once again
A lifeless form, in other life accustomed dear,
But now a carrion, linen-shrouded thing
It knew not, felt repulsion for.

"Lazarus, come forth!"
Had command been made again,
Or were the ringing notes but echoes clear,
Like those returned from stones flung in a
        depthless lake?
The hovering soul, reluctant, could not say.

Transition was so swift,
As swift as flight of swallow borne

From arc of sky to nest by instinct sure, infallible,
So that the soul, thus summoned by
    command omnipotent,
Knew not when radiance of night abruptly ceased,
And dawning pain was stab of earthly light.

"Rabboni, Rabboni mine!"
Had it forced those words from bloodless lips,
Or were they alien, too, as binding scented cloths
That seemed a part of him and yet could not be so?
The wakened creature, now no more a festering
    thing alone,
Resumed its heritage of fleshly joy and woe.

"Rabboni!" thus it made repeat,
As Lazarus, a creature whole and man again,
Faced friend and Lord,
To seek within the eyes of Him adored
The reason for this strange catastrophe
Not met before by any thousand thousand son
Of Adam cursed and loved and saved.

    Mary, He is coming,
    He is down the road,
    Martha, set the fowl to roasting,
    He is near to faint.

Yes, a welcome as a chant had gushed from out
    his throat;

A dozen times and more had he chanted
    greeting words,
When the mighty Prophet's voice, the
    Messiah's voice,
Was crystal heard above the song of homing birds,
Laughing heard on sunset hills of Galilee.

    And Martha, sister Martha, pious plain,
    Had set the fowl to roasting on the spit,
    Hurried then to make the cakes of barley;
    All those preparations a guest to entertain
    Had Martha made, as shout went up and
        down the lane,
    That Jesus, son of David, prophet mighty,
        prophet unafraid
    Was near, might house with them again.

    And Mary, sister Mary, was her soul
        without her then,
    That she swooned in ecstasy,
    That she cared not how the fowl was turned,
    Or the cakes of barley made or the
        honey strained
    Could it be that she and she alone perceived
    How the mighty Prophet could bring this
        agony to me?

    Rabboni, was it for this we told the stars,
    The while sweet Martha filled our plates,

And Mary leaned against Your knee,
And we three forgot that marts, bazaars,
Conquerors harsh their toll would always take?

A dove in the dusk, low and throaty low,
Was Your voice, Rabboni, now I know,
Such was Your voice, husky, dove in the dusk,
Full of love, full of pain's wearied musk,
Such was Your voice that night
When You supped, when You stayed,
When You told of the stars till the light
Grayed on the hills of Galilee,
Such was Your voice.

Ah Rabboni, what of the night
In the tomb wherein I was laid?
But more what of the light You vouchsafed
        I should see,
That light which eyes human and pupiled
        in flesh
Recognize not till eternity,—
Of that state of becoming what shall I say,
If mention I should that indescribable day?

The soul wakens but the flesh is still cold,
The muscles stiff, corded and stiff,
And the eyes green-gangrenous, weary and old,
They are loath, those eyes green-gangrenous to
        waken and see

The marts, the bazaars, the world-ravished dark
In an age-ancient throe of hatred and woe.

    Rabboni, must I waken and see?
    What purpose serves now
    This darkness from light
    To which You thus summon me?
    And now this command You've placed on
        my lips,—
    It shall not be mine, however I wish,
    To speak of the darkness, the sun's bright eclipse,
    That was light and was knowing, was
        unutterable bliss.

Martha, come near, you the dear one of earth,
My hand in your palm calloused hard hold
    comforting close,
My hand still throbbing with pangs of unwanted
    new birth,
So that I forget, if for one moment I may,
That long frightening journey,
That final and glorious combat with death.

And you, Mary, to you there is little to say,
For you understood always, my sister who chose
The bread and the wine of sacrifice sweet,
The ways of doing and giving peculiarly yours,
Discerning while young that selfishness needed
To transcend the exactions of lesser allures.

Yes, I come,
I am coming at once,
As soon as a greeting I give
To neighbors most fearful, perplexed,
And soon as a look I take round
At a world so familiar, so childishly vexed
By problems of ploughing and planting
        and scheming,
By polities new, though ancient as those
Of our Abraham sire;
While the sun on the ridge is gold as always,
And the morn ever dewy matin with praise.

Yes, Rabboni, I come at gentle command,
Though loath I may be.
But may I ask now in this moment
Of unwanted new birth,
This assuming again the burden of man,
Why have You called me
From home You have made,
High-arced beyond light of latest born star,
Back here to earth which now seems to me,
Since mankind's longest last journey
Has been mine to achieve,
The darkest of darkest abyss?

The Questing Self

That secret agony of doubt,
In lair within my inmost self,
Reptilian from depths comes out
When azure dyes the sky again.

Not trustful like the creature blind
To all but instinct's true command,
The coaxing joys that years unwind
To satisfy each innate need,

The winter darkness of my soul
Peers forth at brilliant April skies
To ask, could beauty be the goal
For clay cursed with a questing self?

Passing Through Iowa

A gray farmhouse leaning against the unquiet hill
    of winter,
Its poplars bending to the winds' uprooting touch,
Its morning-glories whispered memories on snowy
    steep of porch,
And the breathing of its shrouded loveliness
    an agony
In the strangling clutch of the murderous cold;
A smothered veil of smoke rising from its chimneys,
And alien arabesques on windows that once kissed
The bright serenity of a summer's morn;
A whiteness vast on fields that loved the green
Of promise and fruition's mellow gold.

Not strange, perhaps, from bleak cocoons of
    other winters,
Except for those lines of young men, at
    every station,
Tall as ripe corn, waiting for those disused
    wooden cars
Now put to use, that would take them, those
    tall young men,
Tall as the golden corn, stalwart as the golden grain
Of their native state, to the wars they had not made.

This was Iowa as we went through in a year of history,

To come on a coast turreted with guns aimed
    at the skies,
Where the skies would soon be rent by that which
    no gun
Of golden son from state of golden grain
    could combat.

Parallel

You have not seen the cactus grow
And blossom on the desert white,
For if you had you might forget
The blood in Europe's darkest night.

For then your doubting anguished soul
Might find this simple parallel,—
That where is seeming harshest waste,
There glows a flower immortelle.

Lidice

The sickle gleamed like whetted moon
In rippling grass, tall-thistled field;
The sickle swung too close, too soon,
Where swayed the linnet's choired nest.

One cleaving arc and choir was stilled,
A home despoiled and fledglings lost,
A world in wreck, hearts terror filled,—
But birds, they say, can build their world again.

Somewhere

Somewhere I know is altitude
Where penguins might flamingoes be,
And Arctic bergs of bluest ice
Contract to grains of golden certitude.

Somewhere are woods of whitest birch
Where little ones, Franciscan loved,
And souls of minted, Christ-stamped worth
Asylum find, free from all search.

Carolina Prelude

The rain spun webs among the dogwood trees,
To make a symphony of silver mist,
Compound of burgeoning spring and winter freeze,
A crotchet now of whine, reluctant whist.

The silver symphony was woodwind kissed
With softly tinkling contrapuntal hopes,
As sun wooed gentle rain and wind wooed mist
Between the dogwoods' glistening spider ropes.

The sun once briefly touched the budding trees,
To sigh above the boughs a sheen of gold,
For buds become the marriage bed of bees,
As years grow young and men and wars grow old.

From a Winter Window

Green they are, seen through their meager
    coverlet of snow,
waxen green, as if the substance of their
    being ebbed,
receded in some strange unknown throe;
motionless they rest, frozen-still to wrack of time,
while stubborn oak leaves cling like thwarted hopes,
cry out defy, then fall in ghostly pantomime.

Old-fashioned flowers these, that lie beneath
    the snow, ·
beneath those towering trees, stalwart grim to
    season's might,
they were named "Sweet William" in an era
    long ago;
long before the scientists chlorophyll had found,
long before they knew an atom is more potent
    than the sun,
long before men feared the secrets of the earth
    they had unbound.

So still Sweet Williams lie in this the winter of
    atomic snow,
they seem to know not they, but man, shall be
    the first to go.

The Willows Arched Their Gold

The willows arched a haze of gold
Along the greening river bank,
Their elfin lift disdained the old
As spring's elixir greedily they drank.

Below the bank the river strove,
As currents south met northern flow,
To shake off ice of winter wove,
And go, perforce, as season bade it go.

But as I watched this battle won,
I thought of nations, my own heart,
And wondered what great thing and lone
Might give us both some new and signal start.

My heart was ice-locked to life's stream,
As, well I knew, the fearsome world,
And both were searching for the sign "redeem,"
That might somehow, somewhere be loft unfurled.

It has not come, that sign "redeem,"
Though spring casts out its willows gold;
No nation trusts another one's esteem —
How can we ransomed be from winter's cold?

So Much Loveliness

So much loveliness without the sight,
So little love within,
How reconcile the Cereus of night
With selfish universal sin?

So rich tall grain lands glean the light,
So hungry peace-time's child,
When shall the world begin to fight
A conscience smugly isled?

Peace

A thousand feathers grayed the sky,
A pæan rang as birds dropped over,
The while some sadly joyful men
Ploughed up remains of fields' dead clover.

At last on native soil, back home
They were, now war was vanquished winter;
They hymned aloud till plough struck mine,
And men and birds knew peace together.

Illusion Moderne

I saw tall soldiers
helmeted against the sky;
suddenly to my alarm
there seemed a score or more —
gigantic enemies in battle khaki dress,
a sight to strangle breath, engorge the eye.

But then as eyes accustomed grew
to autumn light,
I knew myself, as lately, spelled
in dusk's illusioned snare —
there was no regiment of soldiers
there upon the hill,
only oaks with converged crowns,
each one, nature's knight.

Contemplation

He was an old monk, brown and seamed,
Of features peasant strong;
And his habit brown with cowl of same
Was wrinkled, too, as if throughout the night
He had not slept,
But instead, had kept some vigil solitary
With a lonely solitary star,
Seeing in that body luminous,
That planet one and lone,
The counterpart of his own soul.

He did not sit,
But rather sprawled his lean, ascetic frame
Upon that choir bench,
Among those carved and apostolic stalls,
Devoid of worshippers except himself;
His great gnarled hands lay lax
On texture rough of robe,
His face, impassive as a copper coin,
Was profiled to the aisle wherein I crept
To rest again a tired, a worldling's sight
On famed and ornamented glass,
Aglow and richly blue, ethereal
In sunset's light.

The minutes passed, and from the pew

That I had chose for view
Of windows unsurpassable for sensuous delight
In figuration, color's sheen,
I cast a glance occasional,
Curious and speculative at monk
Upon that choir bench, so still
He might have been a sculptor's vision sunk
In marble block, some granite ancient brown
Impervious to fact that time can wean,
Can win all things, men and even rock
From place of birth, from holiness, renown.

The planes from Treasure Isle
Were thundering overhead
On routine practice flight,
And colony of birds, in live oaks' arch,
Were plucking strings of pulsing throat
Whenever chimed caesura from the
          disciplining planes.

He did not seem to note the war-like roar,
The songsters' violent ecstasy,
The moment's silence in between them both,
That monk, marble-fitted into choir bench,
Sunk in converse intimate with God.

And then, deep in those monastery walls,
There sounded five long peals;
A summoning bell to prayer, I thought,

And waited, at that moment still as he
Who only sat and silently adored his Lord,
Most holy of contemplatives, I told myself,
And watched to see what he would do.

Slow as a hyphen mark in speech,
A white clad monk
Formed drift through sanctuary door,
The first of long and ghostly white processional,
Proceeded, gave a genuflection low
At altar, roundly purple now as dried up wound
In light poured from those windows sensuous,
Then slowly came with measured pace,
With hands peaked tall and lowered head
Toward those apostolic stalls
To claim his place.

The old and brown and wrinkled monk
Rose up and made a bow,
Profound, obeisant,
Wrapped robe about his lean, ascetic loins,
Then quickly strode away to shop
Or kitchen task or garden chore,
His hour of freedom passed,
His time of recreation o'er;
For as he disappeared through small-cut
        chancel door,
I knew him finally as brother lay,
An humble one, not churched nor sanctified,

Anointed not to chant that canticle,
Ecclesiastical ordained, thanksgiving to
    creation's Lord,
As day is folded on each dark or shining particle,
And malely hymned to rest.

Myself

Small circle of myself I am,
God made of me,
When unto me was given life;
No diameter can measure me,
No circumference compute my strife;
And never constant may I be,
For I am but a molecule
Within creation's plasmic sea
Where other molecules drift close,
Sometimes flow over me,
Or else absorb a part of their own selves
Into my fluid entity;
But still I strive to be
That little circle of myself
God made of me.

Induct

Oh, how should one begin to know
That moment quiet, wondrous, lone,
As sharply felt as impaled thorn
Upon a sacrificial head,
Signal bright as potent force
That stirs to waxen breathless bloom
The lily pad in recessed miry bed;
A moment such as saints must know
When You are pain, and You are sun
From out the depths of crackling flame
To sear to loveliness Your own?

Chalice

Cup within Your hands my futile life,
And of Your clasp a golden chalice make,
In which there can be poured each hope, mistake,
And sin of this my constant, earthly strife;
A time or two I've felt Your dart, Your knife
Of probing sweet; the greater ache
When You seemed cold as frozen prism flake,
Elusive as the pheasant's mating fife;
But all my yearnings will not bring You near,
Nor chant of birds that winter-gleaned my grain,
Nor bloom of bulbs that knew my autumn care;
Not one of us nor all can make You hear
Unless You mint for us a chalice rare,
And pour Your creatures' love in cup's domain.

Poem

A poem is not made
The way that men drink wine,
With laughter and with gust.
A poem breaks the dam
Of one's own self
Because it wills, because it must.
There is no why,
No answer known
For burst of words that seek,
That hope to be the voice
Of Him unheard. Perhaps, one dawn
The poet listened
To a thrush that stirred.

To the Holy Ghost

This was the thing but few men knew
And none had told to me,
Though seers had planted seed of it
Within their philosophic plots,
In vain to bring to fullest bloom
The wonder inescapable it was;
And only saintly souls had heard it tongued
Within the woods of mankind's soul;
Until one night the Pentecostal flame
Was bright above the fields
As nature bowed, the greening wheat,
The budded trees, the blossoms of the spring,
While thunder echoed on the hills;
And in their nests the birds were still,
And in the pond the frogs had muted basso strings,
As lightning silver-smited all the land—
Then, and only then, I knew the force
By which all creatures live,
Or else succumb to nothingness.

The Hour Glass

You cannot stop it;
turn the glass up,
turn the glass down,
shake it from side to side,
you cannot stop it;
that slow inevitable trickle of time.

You are there in the glass,
you are sand in the glass,
imprisoned even as it,
grain by grain you must live,
grain by grain will you fall
in the fast noiseless rhythm of time.

The Essence

          This hour,
that is a crystal miracle
within itself,
is all I have,
and all I need to have
that I may know
not some other hour,
nor some distant day,
is globed perfection
and separate unity of being
which we call time.

          This hour,
this moment then is mine,
to take within myself,
if I would learn
the mystery of me and it,
and know myself not lost
but possessed in it;
for if I had a thousand such,
no more nor less of being
would I know
than I know now.

Progress

Words so wondrous simple they might be sand,
Light, golden and ephemeral,
Sand sieved in claws obscene of seeking crab,
Light spumed by waves' regardless hand,
Dictates wove of mist in green asexual trees,
That globed a thousand, thousand living spheres
Ten thousand dreams in futile miniscule,
To silver splinter in their mysteries,—
Those were Your deathless words in Galilee.
They did not understand. How could they then,
Those men so recent harsh arboreal,
As anthropologists now pitying see?
Arboreal yet might seem the men of atom's skill,
As sand Your words in mind of fiendish kill.

Lost Grace

You asked me in, not once,
But many times You asked me in
To warm myself before Your fire.
I should have heeded Your request,
For were You not my landed squire?
But ever, for some cause or other,
I minded not Your invitation.
One time, I thought, in my young pride,
Mere fools attend Your convocation,
More worldly company I sought;
One other day it seemed a fire
Was needless in the spring ripe breeze,
A useless winter rite to tire
Those pained with moralistic ease.
Occasions other I recall:
A whispered word outside Your gate,
Your smile more brilliant than the fall;
I shrugged at autumn, my own fate.
And then last night when wailed the storm,
And chosen friends and I lacked wood,
I saw Your hearth fire blazing warm,
But found a bolted door — and understood.

The Search

I sought to sight Your face on land or sea,
in galaxies of space,
then hoped to find Yourself at least revealed
in rhythms proved of nature's grace;
pursuant still I pondered known rules
by which the countless elements combine
to form themselves and all that lives and grows
in patterns deemed of mind divine.

Proud God, how You eluded me!

Still confident I sought You in the town,
intensity in look,
as though each passing, heedless one
might be Your etched or ciphered book;
I knew I had not found You here nor there,—
adversity of human pride,
so mocking spied beneath white wimpled shield,
at last to see You verified.

Pure God, how You defrauded me!

Carrousel

The wind whirls through, the wind whirls round
each mellowed autumn street;
a leaf blows here, a leaf blows there,
on wings perverse and fleet.

A thought whirls through, a thought whirls round
my carrousel of mind,—
a deed is winged, a grace is missed,
mine nevermore to find.

Holy Skepticism

Steep myself I shall in ancient lore,
Ancients' wisdom grasp to breast;
Some may ask, why, whatever for?
Some may say, that brings not rest.
Concede to both of friends I must
The right to fling a scornful nay
To mankind's aged, sanguine trust,
To ghost of father, righteous, fey.
I do not hope to know the why
The oak leaves turn from gold to rust,
Nor listen thrush to certify
His flight from summer's yellowing dust;
But still the ancients' mellow lore
I'll seek as years amass their leaves
Upon my wearied spirit core,
Some answer find — Before the sheaves!

Challenge

Had we the sight, the will to keep
Within our heart, without dismay,
The constant newness of each day,
Its magic challenge, pure and deep,
Then death, we'd know, is not decay,
But moon obscured in shadowed sleep.

Pendulum

This One
I've found since many years of doubt
In singing sough of wind in autumn trees,
In birds' first sleepy chimes as light
Grayed on the brim of cosmic bowl,
In cadenced fall of freshening rain
Upon a greening anxious field;
Sweet sounds and gentle, all of them,
A harmony and rhythm that knows no scale.

This One
And still, I've heard as moon-enchanted surf
Replied in rolling thunders on some rocky beach,
Or as rampaging chemicals of air
Sent splintering fire to rend and tear;
Sounds of terror, sounds of mournfulness,
Emphasizing human loneliness.

Beyond all this, the mystery and the silence
In solitary prison cell of earth,
The bars at windows and the whimsey of the light
In gleams occasional upon the prisoner gaoled;
So were it not for what I like to term
God's pendulum of sound,
That moves in moods and periods measureless,
That now delights and soothes with dulcet notes

And now peals out in awesome power,
This cell of being could not contain me,
Somehow I would be gone from it.

This One

I now assure myself, in sovereign scheme,
Precision mathematical,
Had set the clock of universe to silent beat,
And then, with prescience of man's loneliness
Mid coils of spinning other worlds,
Compassionately a pendulum of sound attached,
With hopeful thought that it might serve
As His own speechless voice,
Attuned to only spirit ears.

The Better Thing

The doe came down to darkling water's edge,
With aspirant anguished breath and heaving side,
To there stand motionless by rocky ledge,

In all that wilderness no place to hide
From enemies, so filled with purposed greed
They kept no sanctuary sanctified.

She knew their form, their signs, their alien breed,
She knew they sought her doom by searing thing
That fought no fight before achieving deed.

Her head sank lower still at lift of wing,
As heron blue rose from the sunset lake
To leave her to the hunter's hungering.

Sigh not, oh doe, it is but little ache
Death brings, compared to living fear, heart-break!

Prerequisite

Before I could know You,
and know You I never shall,
inside of me I know now, I should be
as meadow all stripped of pasture or rye,
a field wanton wet for refuge of wings,
a desert gold arid for wine of Your rain,
that I should be
before I could know You;
a waiting of roots for command of Your sun,
the throat of a thrush stilled
for the call of Your lute;
only a wasteland in darkness,
my dykes purple filled full
with love and with longing,
tumid with longing and the night's star eclipse,
that should be the self of myself
before I could know You.

Shadows

The apple blossoms, spindrift fall,
To foam a schottische on the grass,
A palely eager springtide sun
Bows arc through which they pass.

A hawk, a crow drop cloak to ground,
And shrill the darkness of their stay;
The sun enraged flouts forth his power,
Obliterates their roundelay.

But Lazarus, in mankind's common tomb,
A lengthening shadow cast on rock,
Until the Christ bowed fact to hope
And Lazarus sang matins with the cock.

Young Kathryn

Veronése gold the sunset shone
on planes of lifted face
where young Kathryn sat,
and there two merging lives were met
in amber traceries, faery fine.

The sunset gilt did not obscure
(or so it seemed to me
who watched with jealous eye)
the morning's figuration that anoints
like saving oil the soul that's lately sprung
from thought of fecund Infinite;
but rather did it there enhance
the shy and ardent eagerness with which
our Kathryn's wakening self
gave welcome to an alien world.

They joined, those two-fold lives,
while day scrolled fugue unto its dying hour,
and maiden lifted glance of saint contemplative
to one that typified experience
and subtle sin and proud achievement,
man conceived and man matured.
Like strangers met at turnpike branch
or happenstance in village inn,
the life of sentient bird or beast

that hers had been till then
sloughed natal innocence to know
this other life, whose intimate
she could not help but be
till once again her self
was quit of choice in some far galaxy.

So in a shaft of Veronése gold
a childhood ceased;
some there are that end in ugliness,
and some, in beauty meet.

Peter
To His Lord

I am that certain print
Your foot made in the sand;
Turn You and look at me,
Extend Your loving hand.

Had You not come that day
I still would be smooth sand
Upon the shore, no mark
On me, and no command.

Trusteeship

The lovely helpless things that God has made
And left in trust to mankind's errant care,—
How shall their count begin, what legends trace
To near approximate their score?
And how shall estimate be judged
Of dower, Spirit-trusted, flesh-disposed?
Should same commence with lowly desert flower,
Or polyp coral on ocean shore?
Perhaps a century plant in holy hour
Of bloom might give significance;
Or else a salmon spawning to its doom
Perverse to stream and ordained fate,
An orchid clinging to the jungle's gloom
Would illustration somehow make;
A fawn, in frantic search of mother breast
in forest-filled with rifle-harsh refrain,
Might mark how man has kept this trust.
But child of slums in kindred's court,
Condemned as foe of righteous church and state,
Bereft of love, all filial support,
Could best this illustration make.

Some Things Remain

Some things there are that shall the same remain,
In hour of thought, in age of time's set clock,
No matter what the tongue, the note, the pain
By which they fasten selves to instinct's rock,—
Some things there are that shall the same remain,

A jonquil bright defying April's frost,
A rose that pours its blood to fullest bloom,
Though drought may ask a savage wanton cost,
The tree that jousts its golden shield to doom,—
These things there are that shall the same remain.

The star that blazes for an eon but to fall
In trailing holocaust to stranger earth;
A flight of geese obeying mating call
And snaring death instead of journey's birth,—
These things there are that shall the same remain.

But what of you, my doubting love, and me?
Have we denied that early blighting frost,
The middle years of hope's fecundity,
Those autumn days we knew we were but dust,—
Do we own now the One that shall remain?

Ever After

The silence of nothingness
enfolded all the world
when you had left;
nothingness, complete and final
enfolded every leaf and tree and flower,
and my heart, too, knew no life,
no sustenance, no bloom, no beat
when you had left;
over all was stillness bound—
it was nothingness, complete and final,
deadness, and no stirring after;
though into that wasteland came a solitary note,
and the dead wasteland heard—
a harsh cry, soon swiftly over,
the carrion crow on wing to prey.

Bargaining

The fabric fabulous, that men call life,
I'd yield to you, the weaver bold,
entrepreneur of the warp and woof,
the spinner skilled in daffodils of gold,
forsythias in needle-pointed bloom,
all hyacinths that rival Virgin's blue,
arbutus hid in woods' rich compost old,
those evergreens that lift a tentative,
a tender, new and greening branch
to sun that's wan from traverse long;
those willows thoughtful as they change
their guise to beckoning of turgid brook—
these springtime wonders all,
these things most dear to me
I'd yield to you without demur
when fabric of my life you've spun,
if you'd but let me make a cover of my own
(a cover wove of all the wrongs I've shed,
a redness for my willing,
a whiteness for the Lord I've bled)
and let me lay it on that plot
you finally assign to me,
so that the Gardener, Weaver of all tapestry
for time and space and love
and earthly bloom,
may know where I am laid
and drop His fructifying tears above.

For Simplicity

It should sing within my head
and yours;
It should be the cello of my heart
and yours,
Else the verse we wing
is not a poem.

It can delve in mystery
but ours;
It can be argument for bread
but ours;
Or thoughts we speak
are vellum dead.

It might be gannet of the storm
but ours;
It might be salvage of the sea
but yours and mine—
Nothing lives unless it sings
to you and me.

Separation

I've often wondered if the rose encounters pain
when she must shed her loveliness,
each petal and each leaf a broken lyre
upon the hard, insensate ground,
no more to catch the ecstasy of wind,
the touch of rain, caress of sun.

I've often wondered if the rose looks down
and feels the bitter wrench of death,
such rue as newly disembodied soul
must taste when it has cast its tegument,
and knows the same consigned to earth,
to lodge therein till resurrection time.

I've often wondered if the one or both
must grieve because its other self is gone,
no more to see the tender whorl of spring,
the pageant grace of summer fields,
but more the sunlight warm in lovers' eyes,
that tribute to its vested loveliness.

Yes, certainly, both rose and soul must feel
a separation consummate.

Largesse

May the great hunter, lone and inescapable,
come upon me unaware,
soft-stalking as one would the deer;
not from fear, not that I am more culpable,
perhaps, than most his daily quarry,
not that I hold in such passionate esteem
this life which I must forfeit;
not that living years have dealt me misery
too weighty for this spirit frail,
too insupportable
for this squeamish human flesh to bear,
do I pray the great hunter
may come upon me unaware.

Is it lack of courage then
to test the substance and the mystery
of his dark and secret snare,
or stubbornness of prideful will
that would deny myself as prey
the same as bird or hare,
which goad me to implore
this largesse of surprise?

Somehow these reasonings do not satisfy,
but rather as I ask this boon of him
who will come in his own fated time

to interrupt me in my work,
my pleasure or my sin,
it seems to me my prayerful hope
must rise from out the wisdom of that very earth
of which so long I've been a part,
or else from inborn subtlety
within recesses of that other self
which came to sojourn here awhile,
then willingly or not to stranger spheres depart.

Whatever be the source of this my wish,
I beg the hunter great
to make for me transition brief,
one moment to be caught
in bondage to the earth,
the next, in snare of safe Infinity.

Autumn

The days are hazy now
with fogs like feathers over Tamalpais,
the sun is warm to challenge teasing tempers of
    the wind,
the Bay is gray except where currents sweep
to meet the ocean's colder blue;
at night the stars possess a fiercer light,
and Orion rides a trail into the deepening wood;
the butterflies are back again,
not summer visitors, but adventurers wide-winged
from jungles strange
that man in all his scientific skill
has never yet explored
nor limned on map nor chart;
the humming bird is rarely still,
as spirit lost it searches for its need,
which like God's smile to contrite soul
must come when penitential solstice is complete
in fervent fruitfulness;
meanwhile the days are hazy, gray,
and fogs like whispered prayers
rest over Tamalpais.

The Woods Tonight

The woods tonight
are whitely distillation
of all Your willful loveliness
and pride;
the trees, the evergreens
are sheathed, grimly stark
in icy decimation,
as moon skis high
on slopes of clouds bemused.

The streets tonight
are bluely punctuation
of all Your seeming thoughtfulness
and care;
the alleys, rookeries
are still, hungry dark
for ready degradation,
as vulture screeches cry
on steep of freedom gaoled.

The Skein

One sits, one thinks—
give me a skein
to unravel my brain
in sequence of two and three;
one, two, three, purl,
or has the hank spun out?

One thinks, one sits—
give me a field
to plough as willed
in furrows of marl or loam;
God! there's a skull bleached white!
when was the land ploughed out?

An ALVED *Publication*